A 31-Day Prayer Journal

RELATIONSHIP WITH HIM

This is for those who have allowed situations
in life to take them away from Him.

by
Christie McKinney-Evans

Relationship with Him
Published in Boston, MA by WMS PRESS

For any ordering information or special discounts for bulk purchases, please contact christie@m5womenministries.com

Relationship with Him

By WMS PRESS

1st edition, Dec, 2018
Printed in Boston, MA

DEDICATION

To everyone that has been a part of my life big, small, good, bad, happy, or sad, taught and learned on this journey from the North, South, East and West, THANK YOU! Thank you!

THANK YOU! To my children that God entrusted me to mother; Terika, Brandon, Alexis, Morgan & Gregory who have taught me how to love and cherish every moment of memories in our Relationship, and that family over everything is worth it all. To my mother Benoit, I thank God daily for building and strengthening our relationship as mother and daughter and as believers of the Kingdom. My auntie, Charita from the late phone calls, prayers and working for the Kingdom, my heart is full of gratitude.

To my sister, Stacie thank you for our journey of life to be all that Abba Father has designed for us to be as we continue to strive for the high calling of Jesus Christ. To my beloved Granny, the late Rev. Mary Armanda Wilson who left a legacy and a mission on my life; that has taken me all these years to say yes. To my god parents, spiritual mothers, leaders, coaches, mentors, pastors, apostles, bishops who God put in my life before the foundation of the earth to complete the vision and purpose encouraging me and telling me that I AM a World Overcomer, Walking in Dominion, Christ is my Rock, while living in my Jubilee.

To my king of Destiny and Purpose, Pastor Vernon E. Evans, what can I say…. Thank you for encouraging me, pushing me, sacrificing our time and allowing me to hear Abba Father and the Holy Spirit guide me as an author, ministry and most of all my journey of a 'Relationship with HIM', our Lord and Savior Jesus Christ.

INTRODUCTION

This book is dedicated to every person who has been in a relationship and it did not turn out the way they imagined or maybe it did. The lesson I have learned and still continue to learn is that our number one relationship must be with the Father; because we were created to have daily commune with Him, just like Adam and Eve before the fall.

In Genesis 3:8-9 Adam and Eve walked in the cool of the day with God (daily fellowship) as we were created to do the same, God begin to call Adam, "Adam, Adam where are you?" Just like Adam sin keeps us from hearing and walking with Him daily. Once Adam and Eve ate of the forbidden fruit, they knew they had sinned, and they covered their sin of disappointment with fig leaves. How many times do we cover ourselves in the sin of _____ (only you and God knows), then we run and hide from Him? Once we hide the enemy will continue feed you a lie. This book was birthed from my journey of falling in love with Jesus who has and is still showing me daily that the most important relationship I can have is with Him.

Let us Build and Strengthen our Relationship with Him, Our Lord and Savior Jesus Christ, in this 31-Day Prayer Journal. You will fall in love with Him and begin to develop, create and nourish your personal Relationship with Him.

ACKNOWLEGEMENTS

My husband, my boyfriend, my lover, and my friend who's always cheering me on and being ok with sharing me with HIM.

My children who constantly told me, "momma you got this!"

My Confidence coach and more, Tina Moore Brown who daily say: "Millions are waiting to hear your story."

My Writing coach Catherine Storing, who prayed, disciplined and push with a spirit of love, compassion, excellence and remind me that, "it's easy, you can do it, because it's in you."

My Mentor Pastor Kimberly Jones (PK), wow... K.I.M. 'Keep It Moving.' She often says: "You were created for Purpose on Purpose." Then she would smile and say, "NO EXCUSES!"

#DREAMTEAM is who they are, who have assisted, encouraged, corrected, disciplined and used their gifts, talents and experiences to help me delivery this baby to many, "Relationship with Him."

Each scripture will take you on a journey of *Building and Strengthening your Relationship with HIM!*

So, as you meditate allow the Holy Spirit to speak to you and share with Him from the foundation of you; watch how your love life blossoms with and in HIM!

Are you ready to get started? Let's go!

TABLE OF CONTENTS

DAY 1 DATE: _____

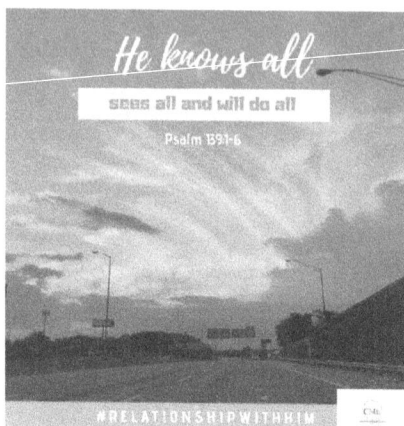

He knows all, sees all and will do all. Psalm 139:1-6, (MSG)

God, investigate my life: get all the facts firsthand. I'm an open book to you; even from a distance, you know what I'm thinking. You know when I leave and when I get back; I'm never out of your sight. You know everything I'm going to say before I start the first sentence. I look behind me and you're there, then up ahead and you're there, too- your reassuring presence, coming and going. This is too much, too wonderful- I can't take it all in!

We are always thinking about how we feel, how someone has treated us, or what has happened in our past. I can remember when there were days that I felt all alone, and no one understood my inner pain of disappointment, discomfort and being emotionally unstable. Who will listen and really understand me or what I was experiencing?

Today take a few minutes and write down 3-5 areas or things you want to share with Abba Father.

DAY 2 DATE: _____

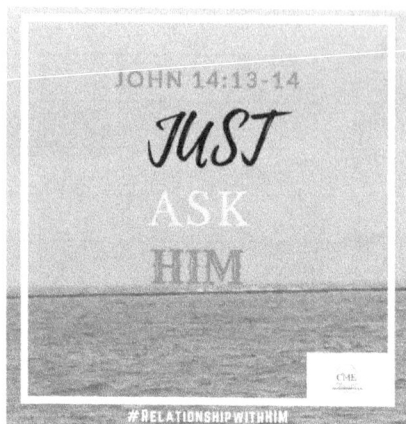

Just Ask! John 14:13-14, (NIV)

And I will do whatever you ask in my name, so that the Father may be glorified in the Son. You may ask me for anything in my name, and I will do it.

There is a wise woman in my life, especially during difficult periods in my life that would always share with me how much God loves me. Even today, I am reminded of our conversations of just how much God loves me and because I am His child, how much more do you think He would give you if you ask? No matter what I may be experiencing today, those words put a smile on my heart and face because of how much Abba Father truly loves me.

Because of a parent's love he/she will do whatever they need to do for their child.

Take a few minutes after reading and meditating on John 14:13-14 and write down 5-7 things you want to ask your Father because you are His child.

DAY 3 DATE: _____

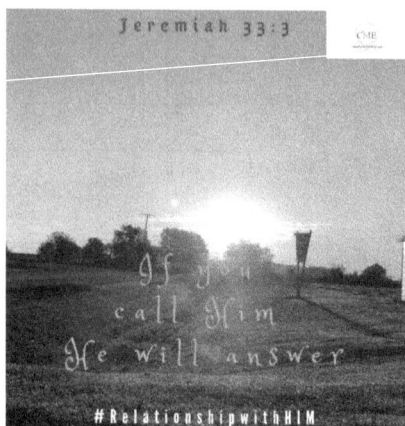

If you call Him, He will answer. Jeremiah 33:3, (NTL)

While Jeremiah was still confined in the courtyard of the guard, the Lord gave him this second message: "This is what the Lord says - the Lord who made the earth, who formed and established it, whose name is the Lord: Ask me and I will tell you remarkable secrets you do not know about things to come.

Normally when someone says they heard a secret about you, this means they will probably never tell you what was said. Then you continually try to do whatever you can to find out what others have said about you. Only when I continued to speak and meditate on this scripture, I realized that no matter what anyone said or the information they might have on me or my past, that the God who created the Heavens and the Earth who formed me could tell me the only secret I really needed to know. What is the secret? He loves me unconditionally.

After meditating on this scripture and your conversation with Abba Father take notes on what He has promised you.

DAY 4 DATE: _____

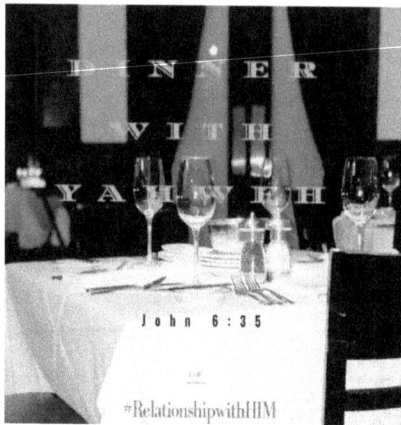

Dinner with Yahweh, Are you thirsty and hungry? John 6:35, (NIV)

Then Jesus declared, "I am the bread of life. Whoever comes to me will never go hungry, and whoever believes in me will never be thirsty.

Thinking back over time when I enjoyed eating a very nice meal at my favorite restaurant; the meal usually gave me peace and comfort, so when I could no longer go, there was a sense of disappointment and sometimes depression. Until, Abba Father gave me a revelation of Him sitting at a table that was set for two and He ask me if I would be willing to join Him? I ask, what did this mean, and He shared, I have been waiting for you to come to me and eat and drink to satisfy the emptiness you are experiencing, and you never came.

After reading and meditating on John 6:35 create a list of 3-5 areas or ways His word will feed your spirit, soul, body and mind.

DAY 5 DATE: _____

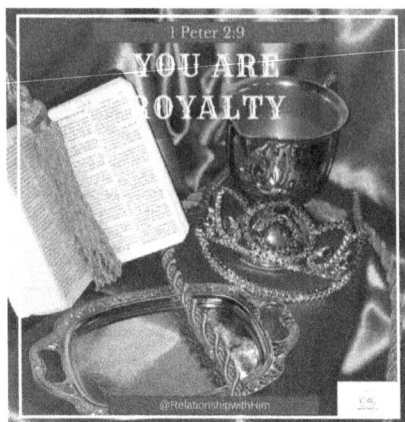

You are royalty, and a chosen people. 1 Peter 2:9, (NLT)

But you are a chosen people, a royal priesthood, a holy nation, God's special possession, that you may declare the praises of Him who called you out of darkness into His wonderful light.

There were moments when I did not think or feel like I was special to anyone other than to God. I often thought: "Will these feelings of being low ever change? You do not know what that is like, or maybe you do.

The more I meditated on the problems the worst things became, until one Saturday during at a Women's Fellowship, one of the speaker's taught with a demonstration. She asked? "What do you do when life gives you lemons? You make lemonade." Sounds so simply and elementary until you sit back and think on it. Only until you change your thinking, know (accept) that you are special, royalty, chosen for greatness, and called for such a time as this will you find inner peace.

How excited are you about being treated like royalty and spending quality time with Him? Write down how you see such time in your head.

DAY 6 DATE: _____

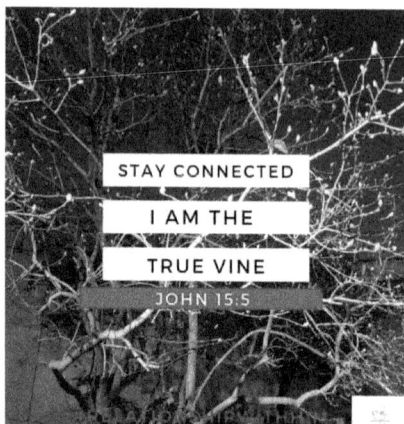

Stay connected, I am the True Vine. John 15:5, (ESV)

"I am the true vine, and my Father is the vinedresser. Every branch in me that does not bear fruit he takes away, and every branch that does bear fruit he prunes, that I may bear more fruit. Already you are clean because of the word that I have spoken to you. Abide in me, and I in you. As the branch cannot bear fruit by itself, unless it abides in the vine, neither can you, unless you abide in me. I am the vine; you are the branches. Whoever abides in me and I in him, he it is that bears much fruit, for apart from me you can do nothing.

I think about my phone charger which is so important to me that I do not go to bed without charging my phone and will go to work and borrow someone else's if I leave home without a full charge. Why? Because I do not want to be without power or to be disconnected from the people I care about. If only we were as diligent when it came to staying connected to our Heavenly Father, but unfortunately we are not. Then He said to me, "Spend time with me and watch the growth, strength and confidence you will gain staying connected with Me."

Make two list of what happens when you charge yourself with the word of God, and list when you don't. How important is it to charge daily?

DAY 7 DATE: _____

Follow His Light. John 8:12, (MSG)

> *Jesus once again addressed them; "I am the world's Light. No one who follows me stumbles around in the darkness. I provide plenty of light to live in."*

Sometimes we are faced with times in our life where seasons come, and we cannot see clearly what God is doing or see our way out. As I type this, I am reminded of several occasions when I did not know which way to go, as if I were driving or walking on a dark road without a flashlight or even knowing how to see. You know God has told you to walk on a certain path, but you do that you cannot see two steps in front of you (that is called a faith walk). But as I continue to seek His Word there is light and hope day after day.

In what areas of your life do you need His light to shine in?

List 3-5 things or areas you want the light of His word to shine on you:

DAY 8 DATE: _____

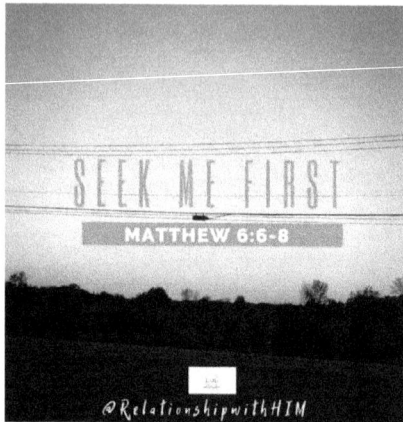

Seek Me First. Matthew 6:6-8, (INT)

*But when you pray, go into your room, close the door and pray to your
Father, who is unseen. Then your Father, who sees what is done in
secret, will reward you. And when you pray, do not keep on babbling
like pagans, for they think they will be heard because of their many
words. Do not be like them, for your Father knows what you need
before you ask.*

We tell everyone how we feel, what's going on in our life, who hurt
us, and the list goes on. After sharing with people, friends or family
members we are still hurt and very often still have no clue as to how to
solve the situation we are in. How many times do we look for others
to give us comfort and understand what we are experiencing and still
have no peace? Take time today, close the door of your heart, remove all
distractions to spend time with Abba Father.

**Abba Father wants you to tell Him first, so tell Him what's in your
heart:**

DAY 9 DATE: _____

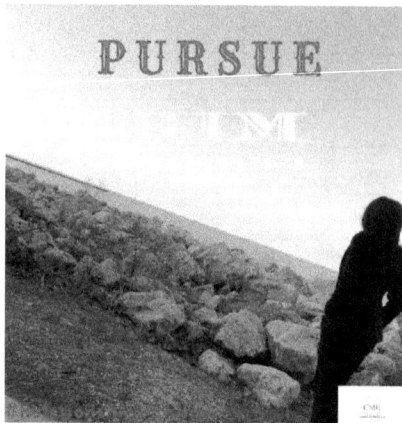

Pursue Him. Psalm 63:1-8, (KJV)

O God, thou art my God; early will I seek thee: my soul thirsteth for thee, my flesh longeth for thee in a dry and thirsty land, where no water is;
² To see thy power and thy glory, so as I have seen thee in the sanctuary.
³ Because thy lovingkindness is better than life, my lips shall praise thee.
⁴ Thus will I bless thee while I live: I will lift up my hands in thy name.
⁵ My soul shall be satisfied as with marrow and fatness; and my mouth shall praise thee with joyful lips:
⁶ When I remember thee upon my bed, and meditate on thee in the night watches.
⁷ Because thou hast been my help, therefore in the shadow of thy wings will I rejoice.
⁸ My soul followeth hard after thee: thy right hand upholdeth me.

When we plant flowers, we can't just plant them and not water them. If it doesn't rain you know that your flowers will need the water hose to look alive. Now, let us think, if we are not seeking Him early or just daily, we will find ourselves dry, slumped over, emotionally drained and the list can go on and on. When you wake up every morning take some time and examine the way your body reacts without drinking anything.

How long can you go without water? Can you list what happens when a person is feeling dehydrated and also, when their spirit man has not spent time with Abba Father?

DAY 10 DATE: _____

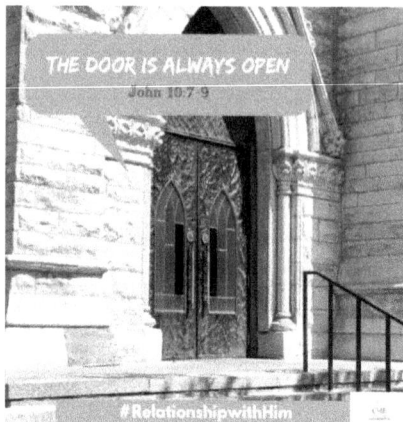

The door is always open. John 10:7-9, (NKJV)

> *Therefore, Jesus said again, "Very truly I tell you, I am the gate for the sheep. All who have come before me are thieves and robbers, but the sheep have not listened to them. I am the gate; whoever enters through me will be saved.*

Whenever we are listening to music, people or watching television, it will get down in our hearts the more we listen to it, or them. I recall a time when feeling disconnected to God, and He said, I had allowed others to speak into my ear who were thieves and robbers. Now that I was a below the belt blow. We must be careful, especially when we are in our lowest moments; we must choose to enter His gate, His arms and His love to hear what He has to say unto us.

Who or what is standing at your door blocking your entrance to deliverance, freedom and destiny? Abba Father's door is always open.

DAY 11 DATE: _____

John 10:3-4
You are valuable, He knows your name

You are valuable, He knows your name. John 10:3-4, (NIV)

> *The gatekeeper opens the gate for him, and the sheep listen to his voice. He calls his own sheep by name and leads them out. When he has brought out all his own, he goes on ahead of them, and his sheep follow him because they know his voice.*

I remember when my grandmother would call my name and depending on the tone of her voice I knew if I was to run or just say: "I'm on my way grandma." As parents when our children call our name, we know by their tone if they need us right away or if they are just calling our names just because. Abba Father knows His children by name and His children know when they call, He will answer.

When you know someone personally you can call them at any time. What do you call Abba Father when you need Him? Make a list of 3-5 names you regularly use and what they mean to you.

DAY 12 DATE: _____

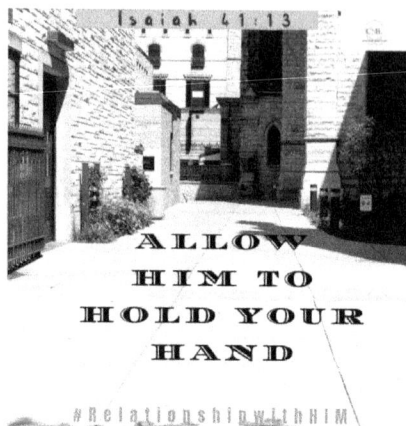

Allow Him to hold your hand. Isaiah 41:13, (MSG)

That's right. Because I, your God, have a firm grip on you and I'm not letting go. I'm telling you, don't panic. I'm right here to help you.

My experience as a single mother: school age children, needing a job, health insurance, a car I can keep adding to the list of things I needed, but I can tell you, prayer was my only place of peace. I would attend noon day prayer at my local church with two amazing mothers of wisdom who would speak hope into my life, and always told me hold on to God's unchanging hand.

Their words of wisdom reminded me of my loving grandmother, I could feel her telling me: "No matter what you are faced with, whatever is in front of you and around you, allow God to hold your hand through it all."

What situation(s) do you need Him to hold your hand through? He is right there to help!

DAY 13 DATE: _____

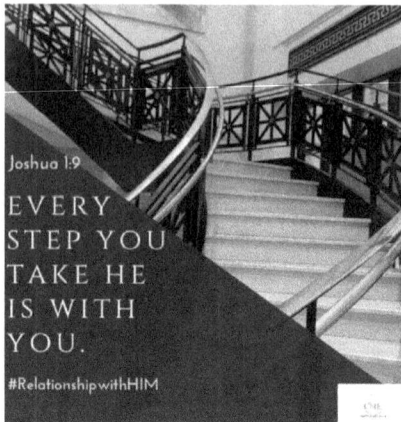

Every step you take He is with you. Joshua 1:9, (GNT)

Remember that I have commanded you to be determined and confident! Do not be afraid or discouraged, for I, the Lord your God, am with you wherever you go."

Making decisions alone, going into new territories, and thinking outside the norm used to be a challenge for me. When God told me to go, do, or approach new things, people or places I was very afraid.

When I needed a job, I told God (yes, I told Him), "Father please open the doors to a place where my passion can be fed, where I can be happy and joyful." I wanted a job where my passion for children and youth would continue to grow. So, God told me to go to the daycare centers and schools in my community by faith and apply, the rest was history.

What new path in your life or business, relationships, family or career do you need to be reminded that He is with you every step of the way?

DAY 14 DATE: _____

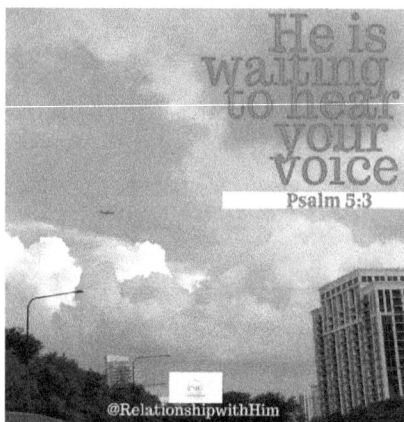

He is waiting to hear your voice. Psalm 5:3, (ISV)

Lord, in the morning you will hear my voice; in the morning I will pray to you, and I will watch for your answer.

Each morning when I go up and before I got everyone ready for their day I would say to myself, "Christie, stop and have your own quiet time; spend time with Abba Father so you are not overwhelmed by what may come your way later today."

There would be days when each child had somewhere to be after school and I had no idea how that would work out, there seem to be not enough time, or enough of me to get everything things done. But listening to His voice for instructions always worked out for my good.

After you are done talking to Abba Father, wait patiently for an answer and write down everything He is saying. Did you ask Him a question, or did you allow Him to ask you a question?

DAY 15 DATE: _____

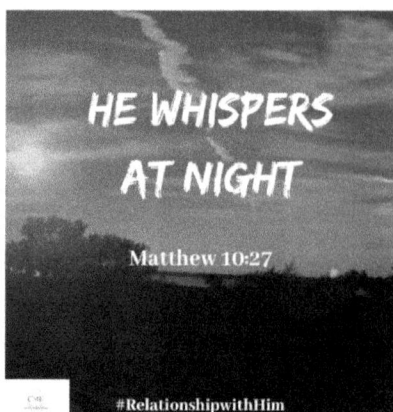

HE WHISPERS
AT NIGHT

Matthew 10:27

#RelationshipwithHim

He whispers at night. Matthew 10:27, (NIV)

What I tell you in the dark, speak in the daylight; what is whispered in your ear, proclaim from the roofs.

When everyone is asleep you are now able to think about your day or just meditate on who, what, when or why this or that happened that day?

After a long day at work or when I needed some quiet time, I remember having pillow talk conversations with Abba Father; those conversations would give me peace and love. It was important for me to make time to speak and listen to my Abba Father. Those conversations prepared me mentally, physically, and spiritually so that I could hear His voice and instructions.

Take this time to lie still and listen to HIM speak to you and love on you as He whispers words of Love, Laughter, and Comfort. Write everything your heart hears and feels.

DAY 16 DATE: _____

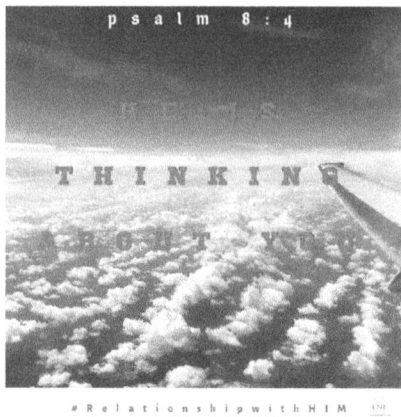

He's thinking about you and coming to visit you. Psalm 8:4, (KJV)

What is man, that thou art mindful of him? And the son of man that thou visitest him?

I longed to be on someone's mind, expecting them to call, text or invite you out to dinner, a movie or just talk was a regular disappointment for me. Then you have thoughts of, "What is really going on that I cannot get a date?" Then God began to tell me that He was hiding me like Moses and He was protecting my spirit, soul, body, mind and my time was to wait on Him. Then He said, "Get dressed because I am coming to visit you!"

I cannot explain my excitement, no one can take that kind of joy away. You have a new outfit, you are groomed the way HE likes, you have on His favorite fragrance and the outfit is popping. Your hair is done to perfection, along with your manicure and pedicure. Now the time has come for the two to meet because He's been thinking of you ALL day and you are both ready for your quality time together.

Are you ready for your date with God? What will you wear? What will you talk about?

DAY 17 DATE: _____

His Word will not return empty or void. Isaiah 55:11, (ESV)

So, shall my word be that goes out from my mouth; it shall not return to me empty, but it shall accomplish that which I purpose, and shall succeed in the thing for which I sent it.

I had my eye on the condo and I first drove around the neighborhood several times, then I went online to see the buying requirements. Nothing I had qualified me for what they were asking for. What did I do? I got in my word, found a scripture and begin to confess His promises. Only then was I able to make a phone call to set up an appointment to see the condo. The first time I saw the place they told me the seller's terms were non-negotiable. I continued to confess, I continued speaking His Word and believing He would give me the desires of my heart. Year two came around and the Holy Spirit spoke and told me to give the agent a call. I met with the agent again and shortly after we moved in.

When you are given specific orders from Abba Father from His Word you expect for them to return with what was promised. You are looking for your request to be answered, and the job to be completed. When we ask HIM for anything and find a scripture to back us up imagine that there is an army of witnesses when you open your mouth to deliver and bring the goods back from HIM to you.

What are you believing Him for, write those things down? Write down 3-5 scriptures to build up your faith, and declare them daily.

DAY 18 DATE: _____

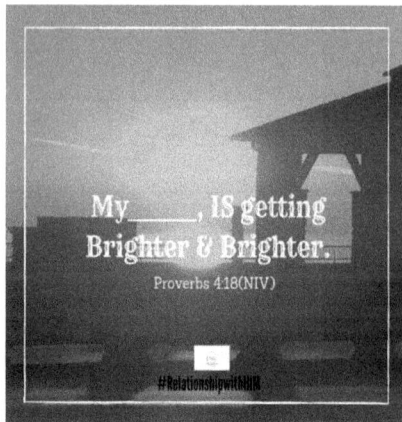

My _____ is getting brighter & brighter. Proverbs 4:18, (NIV)

The path of the righteous is like the morning sun, shining ever brighter till the full light of day.

The more you apply the Word of God to a situation whether a health issue or something to do with your emotions, your vision becomes clearer and clearer which will make your focus sharper and better each time. When asking God to open your eyes so that you may see clear in any situation, because you need clarity quick fast and in a hurry.

When you share your testimony of healing and deliverance to others you find out that until you open your mouth and share, that there is a brighter day ahead for someone else. Imagine a lightbulb, with three brightness settings, as you toggle with the levels your view of the entire room changes, right? In the same way you must think about the stages of deliverance and awareness in your life of healing.

He is reminding you that your _____ (fill in the blank) is getting brighter & brighter because of applying the Word of God.

DAY 19 DATE: _____

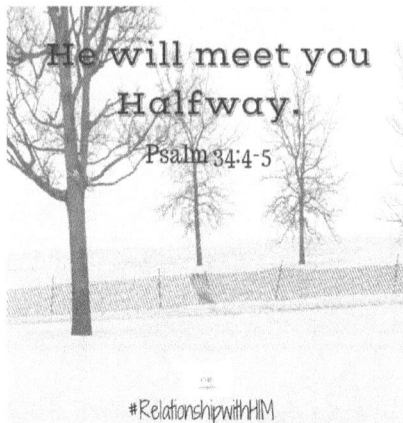

He will meet you
Halfway.
Psalm 34:4-5

#RelationshipwithHIM

He will meet you halfway. Psalm 34:4-5, (NASB)

I sought the Lord, and He answered me, and delivered me from all my fears. They looked to Him and were radiant, and their faces will never be ashamed.

When starting something new; a new journey, or a new race in life you are always nervous before you start. Before track meets our daughter would have a look on her face of determination that her team was going to win. They had worked diligently and were determined to stand firm in what they had practiced repeatedly; they prayed with confidence knowing that they put everything into what they believed.

In a relay race you pass the baton to your teammate and whomever is waiting for it to be passed to them awaits patiently. Now, before you can get tired your teammate begins to meet you halfway to pass the baton. This is how our Father is, He's waiting on you to start walking or running toward HIM! Don't stop now, keep going.

What race, new business, new job or ministry are you starting and need to finish?

DAY 20 DATE: _____

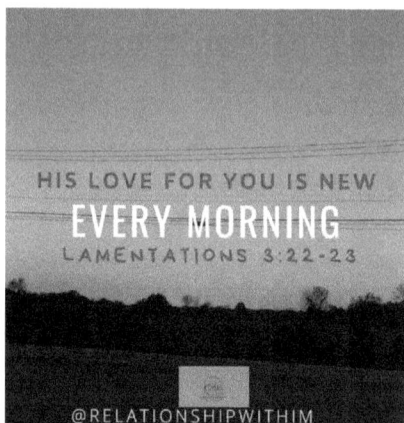

HIS LOVE FOR YOU IS NEW
EVERY MORNING
LAMENTATIONS 3:22-23

@RELATIONSHIPWITHIM

His love is new every day. Lamentations 3:22-23, (MSG)

> *God's loyal love couldn't have run out, His merciful love couldn't have dried up. They're created new every morning. How great your faithfulness! I'm sticking with God (I say it over and over). He's all I've got left.*

Whenever you are at a point in your life that you feel like you're all alone, just know when you are in communication with Abba Father you are never alone. He will remind us every day how much He loves us. How many times do you tell your children, spouses and family members that you love them? Each day we are normally sharing and showing them love in different ways, right? But, when you are experiencing loneliness and the negative thoughts start to replay in your head like a movie, He will quickly remind you of the things we take for granted; HE wakes us up in the morning with the breath of life; that's love, when we open our eyes; that's love, when we wash our face; that's love, when we brush our teeth; that's love, or the strength of the muscles in our body; that's love.

Now, you can add more as the day goes on knowing that His love for you is new every day.

DAY 21 DATE: _____

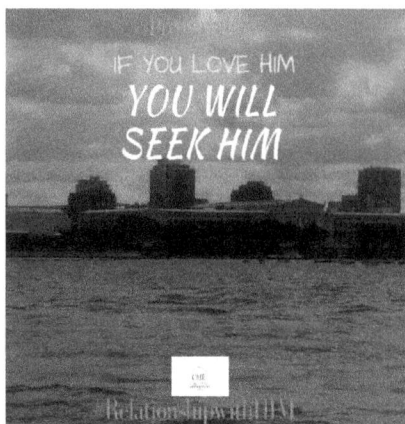

If you love Him. Proverbs 8:17, (NIV)

I love those who love me, and those who seek me find me.

One morning I lost one of my diamond earrings, and was devasted; I was running late and on top of that had an attitude, why? Because I could not find what I was looking for.

How often do we spend extra time looking for something that we are attached to us or holds sentimental value? When a child is missing an Amber Alert can be seen on major highways and television, or if a pet has gotten out of the backyard, the search is on! You grab your flash light, hang posters, make phone calls, and more. Why? Because you care and will do whatever it takes to find them. This is the tenacity we should have when we are looking for HIM and can't find HIM, we must search until we do, because we love Him. Don't stop seeking Him.

How will you seek daily after Him? What are you looking for in your search?

DAY 22 DATE: _____

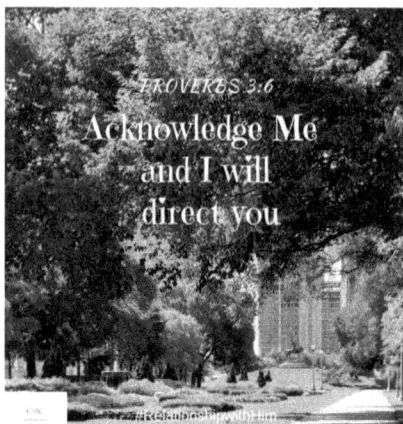

Acknowledge Me and I will direct you. Proverbs 3:6, (NLT)

Seek His will in all you do, and He will show you which path to take.

When someone walks into your house or into a meeting you expect for those in the room to speak or at least acknowledge you, right? This demonstrates home training and proper manners which makes the atmosphere and conversation calm and inviting.

As a single parent I often did not know what to do or where I was headed. This left me feeling lost and insecure.

My emotions became very stressful and my path wasn't clear, a foggy night became a foggy season. I'm sure there have been times you have experience something similar; someone not willing to guide you in the right direction.

Now, today I pray you will acknowledge HIM in your daily plans, life, career and ask Him to guide, direct, and instruct you in the right direction.

Write down what path(s) do you want Abba Father to lead you?

DAY 23 DATE: _____

Bless Him in all. Psalm 34:1, (MSG)

I bless God every chance I get; my lungs expand with His praise.

I love watching my kids play baseball, basketball or dance. I am their biggest cheerleader, screaming at the top of my lungs or you can hear me outside of the stadium. No one can out cheer me for my children, why, because I want them to know that I am there cheering for them. When they see and hear mommy in the stands, they are all smiles and feel confident in that very moment. How do you think Abba Father would feel when He hears our voices thanking and praising Him for all He is doing and has done for us?

What do you need to bless and praise Him for or praise Him in?

DAY 24 DATE: _____

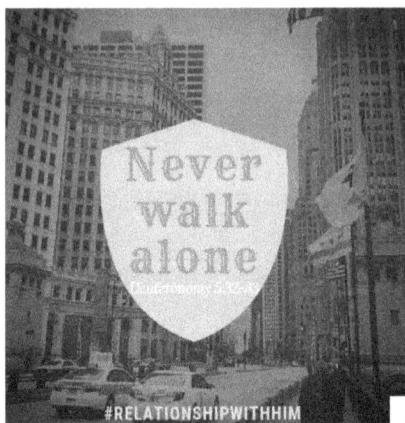

Never walk alone. Deuteronomy 5:32-33, (MSG)

So be very careful to act exactly as God commands you. Don't veer off to the right or the left. Walk straight down the road God commands so that you'll have a good life and live a long time in the land that you're about to possess.

There were many times when I felt as if I was all alone and there was no one to help me with what I was going through. There were days or nights I thought, "How am I going to make it?" When you are alone there are feelings that overtake you, which can leave you very uncomfortable, sad, mentally disturbed and with thoughts that would have your mind all over the place. As you read and meditate on Deuteronomy 5:32-33 you will be reminded that you are never alone, not even in during you lowest times in life.

What areas in your life do you feel that you are all alone? Is it your finances, health, or not feeling loved? Tell Your Abba Father.

DAY 25 DATE: _____

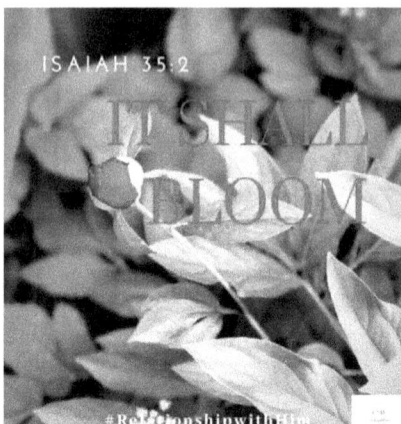

**It Shall Blossom Abundantly; What did you plant in your season.
Isaiah 35:2, (KJV)**

It shall blossom abundantly and rejoice even with joy and singing: the glory of Lebanon shall be given unto it, the excellency of Carmel and Sharon, they shall see the glory of the Lord, and the excellency of our God.

Being angry and upset in life stressful moments will cause you to say things and even think things that are not according to the Word of God. Growing up, my grandmother would say, "Whatever you plant it must come up unless, you are doing some serious praying to cut it from the root." I know that when anger comes, we are so quick to speak how we feel and not what His Word says about our situation.

When you begin to look at your Garden of Life, Garden of Finances and Your Garden of Health it will allow you to see what we have been planting good or bad. Let us begin to fertilize our garden with the Word of God and our Praise of Thanksgiving as water on our Finances, our Health, our Family and our Life.

What are you planting in this season? What do you need to pluck up and plant again the proper way?

DAY 26 DATE: _____

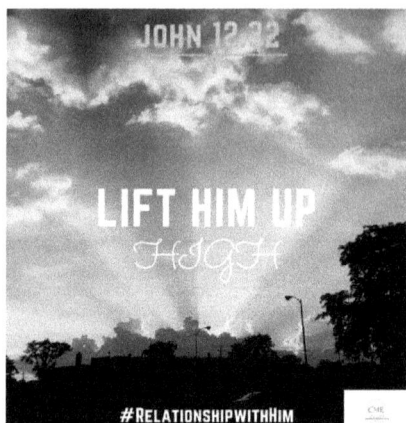

Lift Him up High. John 12:32, (NIV)

And I, if I am lifted up from the earth, will draw all people to myself.

Imagine it's your child's birthday and he or she let the balloons get out of their hands. What happens? Everyone immediately stops and looks up until they can no longer see the balloons, right?

In the same way, how high can you lift Him up today? Lift Him higher than you can lift up your hands. Look up and Lift Him up higher than you can see. There were many evenings I would just sit in my car and look up to the stars and allow the Holy Spirit to speak to my heart. Why? Because it had been either a long day or I just was not in the mood for anything. As I continued to look up at the stars the Holy Spirit would say, "If you lift me up from your heart as high as the stars are, I will draw you closer to me and you will feel my presence close to you, regardless whatever the situation may be."

Take time today and lift up the Name of Jesus who is high above your situation and the stars. What will you lift Him up in praise for today?

DAY 27 DATE: _____

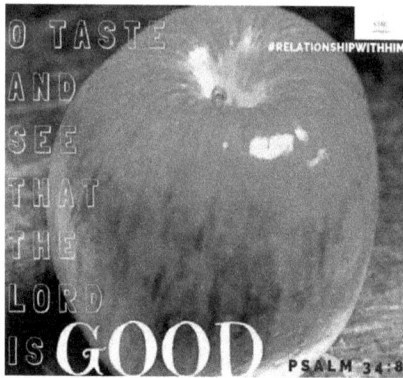

Taste and see. Psalm 34:8, (MSG)

Open your mouth and taste, open your eyes and see-how good God is.
Blessed are you who run to Him.

How many commercials do you see during the Football Season? Every halftime commercial encourages you to try or buy something new, especially during the Super Bowl. Those commercials are so clever and can get you excited and daydreaming about the possibilities, right? The sad part is that those things do not edify our souls or minds.

I remember joining the Praise Team which would take me to a higher place in Him, every time. Because of the commitment I made to be part of the worship team I was reminded during rehearsal and on Sunday morning during sound check that when I open my mouth to praise Abba Father, I would forget about what was so heavy on my heart. Why not get excited about what Abba Father says in His Word about you. Or what His Word says He will do for you? But you must read(eat) His Word to see the results, so you can tell others "O taste and See" what the Lord has done for me!

What part of His word did you eat today? Who will you tell today how great He is to you?

DAY 28 DATE: _____

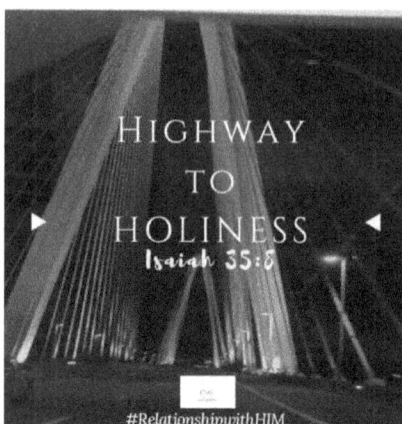

Highway of Holiness. Isaiah 35:8, (NASB)

A highway will be there, a roadway, and it will be called the Highway of Holiness. The unclean will not travel on it, but it will be for him who walks that way, and fools will not wander on it.

When we are planning a vacation, it requires us to get our maps out or use the GPS on our phones or in our cars for directions. If you make a wrong turn your GPS will alert you to turn around or make a U turn at the closest intersection. When you are faced with new seasons in your life and everything is new to you, you begin to ask God, "What direction shall I take in this season of my life?" I would be driving my daily route and look up and be lost because I was not paying attention to the road.

We may think in a normal everyday routine we cannot get lost, but Abba Father quickly reminded me that we need Him to always keep us on the right path of Holiness with Him. Today as you meditate on the Highway of Holiness, in Isaiah 35:8 make sure you are listening to the Holy Spirit signals. "Should I turn around or should I take another route?"

Are you on the right highway(path)? What signals or road blocks do you see?

DAY 29 DATE: _____

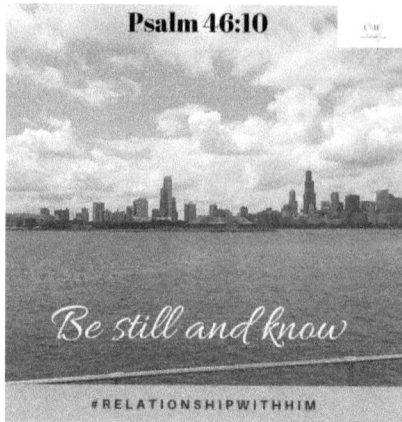

Be still and know. Psalm 46:10, (NIV)

He says, "Be still, and know that I am God; I will be exalted among the nations, I will be exalted in the earth."

In a very busy world or chaotic situation, trust and know that Psalm 46:10 reminds us that Abba Father wants us to, be still and know that He is God. He knows every detail, every issue, every bill, every child by name, every spouse and desire. Why not take a seat and allow Him to give you peace and directions in all of it? My days would be long and busy on top of busy on top of busy. If schedules did not go as planned, I would take time to mentally regroup before going down the path of being frustrated and overwhelmed. Once I was able to sit quietly and I would hear Abba Father whisper very quietly and say, "Be still my child." I would quiet my spirit, soul, body and my mind, and surrender my everything to Him.

What situation(s) do you need to allow God to be God and exalted among the nations and the earth? Do you need to exalt Him above your home, family, businesses, ministry, or work place?

DAY 30 DATE: _____

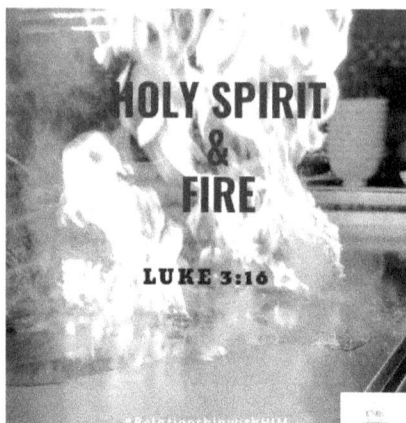

Holy Spirit & Fire. Luke 3:16, (KJB)

John answered, saying unto them all, I indeed baptize you with water; but one mightier than I cometh, the latchet of whose shoes I am not worthy to unloose: he shall baptize you with the Holy Ghost and with fire.

When you welcome someone into your home, you open the door and introduce them to everyone there. Today, welcome the Holy Spirit into your heart, allow Him to spend some time with you today.

The Holy Spirit is a gentleman and when He comes in He is bearing gifts of love, patience, joy, security and happiness. The Holy Spirit also brings Authority and Power with Fire! When He leaves, everyone and everything will know that He was there because of the evidence and love in the atmosphere. Having a relationship and respect of the Holy Spirit is and has been a journey that I could not do without. Many times, when I was in my feelings, "Why me Lord?" He would remind me that some situations require a different kind of power, a different kind of anointing and a different level of sacrifice to allow the Holy Spirit to come in freely.

Welcome the Holy Spirit into the room of your heart, soul, body, mind and whatever situations you may be facing.

What areas of your life do you need the Hold Spirit?

DAY 31 DATE: _____

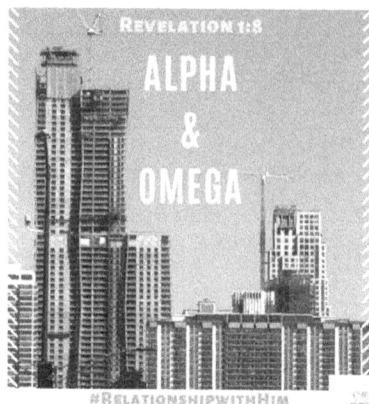

Alpha & Omega. Revelation 1:8, (ESV)

> *"I am the Alpha and the Omega," says the Lord God, "who is and who was and who is to come, the Almighty."*

When building a long-lasting relationship, it could be a business relationship, ministry, marriage or family relationship, it must begin with Abba Father. You may be building or strengthening many things in your life, and when sickness, heartache, financial or relationship struggles occur you know you are determined to win.

Everyday should begin and end with Abba Father no matter what it takes.

As a Child of Our Lord and Savior Jesus Christ, He reminds us that He is Alpha & Omega, the beginning and the end.

What area(s) do you need to give Him? Are you in the beginning or the end?

INVITATION & CONCLUSION

Now, that you have completed the 31-Day Prayer Journal, "Relationship with Him", you can continue with our Spiritual Development Coaching Program that will teach you how to DEVELOP, CREATE and NOURISH your Relationship with Him.

Send us an email for more details to this address: christie@ m5womenministries.com with the subject: I am ready for a genuine Relationship with Him.

As a Relationship Builder, my prayer is that you walk daily with Abba Father as Adam did every day and Build and Strengthen your RelationshipwithHIM Our Lord and Savior Jesus Christ, and Love with the Love of the Lord.

The plan of Salvation Begins With a New Relationship

If you have not accepted Jesus as the lover of your soul and life, read Romans 10:9 AMP out loud.

> Because if you acknowledge and confess with your mouth
> that Jesus is Lord [recognizing His power, authority, and
> majesty as God], and believe in your heart that God raised
> Him from the dead, you will be saved.

Did you read it and did it speak to you? Wonderful! Then, you are now in a New Relationship for Life ☺ Welcome to the Family.

ABOUT THE AUTHOR

CHRISTIE MCKINNEY-EVANS is a Relationship Builder, Motivator and Encourager of the Gospel. She is a License Minister of the Gospel, Prayer Warrior, Worship Leader, Youth Leader, Author of the Book Relationship With Him, and Motivational Speaker.

She teaches and speaks daily on her weekday Facebook and Periscope Relationship With Him Broadcasts. Mrs. McKinney-Evans is also the CEO & Founder of M5 Women Ministries, which inspires women who have given birth to children to also birth a ministry and/or business.

She has served in the ministry for the past 30-years in Tennessee, Arkansas, and Illinois. Her passion is for women who have experienced divorce, single parenting, and are ready to live and love again.

She recently remarried and relocated to Chicago; her birth state. Alongside her husband Rev. Vernon Earl Evans, they serve in the ministry together. Her blended family consists of eight children and six grandchildren.

You can connect with Christie in the following platforms:
https://www.m5womenministries.com/
https://www.facebook.com/RelationshipwithHimCME/
https://twitter.com/mrschristieme
https://www.instagram.com/relationshipwithhimcme/
https://www.instagram.com/m5womenministries/
https://www.periscope.tv/MrsChristieME/

www.ingramcontent.com/pod-product-compliance
Lightning Source LLC
LaVergne TN
LVHW051429080426
835508LV00022B/3306